The Dark Mistress

FIRE WITHIN

Tammy Harrison

FIRE WITHIN

COPYRIGHT ©2014 Tammy Harrison (Dark Mistress)

All rights reserved. No part of this book may be used or permission except in the case of brief quotations embodied in critical articles or reviews. For information address BlaqRayn Publishing & Promotions, 134 Andrew Drive, NC 27320. Copyright infringement may lead to fines under penalty of law as well as other legal actions.

To the best of our knowledge (BlaqRayn Publishing Plus) this is an original manuscript and all written works are the sole property of said author Tammy Harrison.

Printed in the United States of America

ISBN-13: 978-0692345566
ISBN-10: 0692345566

Printed by Createspace in 2014
Published by BlaqRayn Publishing Plus in 2014

Dedication

Poem of dedication to my Dad

A Daughter's Gift

As a child I did not realize

until I was grown

or really never knew, unable to

fully comprehended

How sweet and kind natured you were

or the gentle and wise ways that

I simply took in stride

holding my head high

with foolish teenage pride,dismissing your insightful advise

from day to passing day

All the sacrifices, you made for me

in your own loving way...

But then I grew up and learned

and it finally dawned on me

how much your love has truly meant

how thoughtful and caring you have always been

And so this comes with all the love and gratitude

crashing in waves upon tides of time

I took my time remembering every

Disney Princess stories told, we both new my

secrete dreams I wanted to achieve someday

you deserved more, for a Daughter simply could

not have had a dearer Father...

The Fire Within

Dark Mistress

Mirror, Mirror

Dreams inside of dreams

my memories, portals

of my miserable yesterdays

and past failures

my reflection caught

in the glass and I saw

green-blue hues

that haloed my eyes

and in silence I sat

wondering what lies

beyond the mirror

paralleled possibilities

or is it a mere illusion

of my false light

casting a shadow that

hides behind faded smiles

it looks like me, but it's not

wanting nothing more

than to put my fist

through this mirror

to see what's on

the other side

but subconsciously

knowing it was just

so I would not have to

look at myself anymore,

that and because I thought

maybe I could steal a piece

of glass when no one was

looking and use it to carve

my heart out of my chest

the voices in my head won't

go away so I'm

taking control, she has no choice

to make them stop

she can't be breathing anymore

so there she sits on the floor

with her sharp shiny friend

starting to carve her pain away

layer by layer

feeling the warm trickles of red pain

that are flowing freely from her veins

slowly diminishing and fading to black

so with outstretched arms embracing

the darkness that lingers within

knowing this is the only way

not to be a disappointment

to anyone anymore

Hiding in Shadows

Holding my breath

as life takes its toll

I find myself

in shadows longing

to be with you

I hide behind

smiles living

a life of blue

wondering if

you feel this

hopeless too

I die a little

more inside

each day as

you look away

my heart breaking

in the ocean

of my dreams,

hurting though

I feel nothing

as I touch you

with dead hands

my soul aches

like dark murky

waters in

ambiguous lands

looking at myself

with shamed eyes,

my glance weak,

an ominous voice

lingers.. whispering

I am the dark

side of you

my music is

gone, my ears

are deaf as I

sink deeper

into endless nights

my thoughts are

poisoned ,my mind

insane as I look

in the mirror

my face a death

mask, softly

whispering to myself

mirror, mirror

on the wall

why must am I

the most lonely

girl of them all

Fallen Angel

She fell from the heavens down to this world
Grasping a broken harp
Beautiful white wings now darkest black
Music was a part of her...
Heaven not wanting her anymore
This silence is an endless dream,
Solitude made real in her,
Any trace of warmth in her soul now not there

This Fallen angel, who lost her grace
crying so desperately in the pouring rain
Will you love her under this familiar moon
Under the endless starry sky...
She yearns to fly...
But her broken wings chain her to this earth
Can you free her– with your love
Maybe then her wings will be whole again...

A Fallen angel,
Broken in the worst of ways...

Living in darkest days...
Just listen - don't open your eyes...

She's your fallen angel,
And she cries, so painfully...
She spreads her broken wings, but
Bloody feathers reflect a tainted soul...
She has been alone for many years
Would you ever want to dry her tears...
this fallen angel,
Broken in the worst of ways...
She now lives with her worst fears
please, open your eyes... can you see

She's your fallen angel,
the one you desperately prayed for... now,
she cries, so silently...
she cries, wordlessly...
And she sacrificed her all for you
she heard your plea for love
and fell from the heavens just for you

Soul Searching

I shook my soul

from its secret place

to have a look

And held it up to the mirror

of the mind's eye

As luminous as a star

against night sky

My quivering body

lay in a vast empty space

A spark of pulsating passion

upon my tear stained face

I plunged its darkest depths

and came to see

Why the awful key to my infinity

Conspires to deprive me

Of joy

Of grace

To know the feeling

of beautiful bliss

To wonder if I am blind

To the stirrings of the soul

I looked deeper

than I ever have

To find the core

I discovered a new way to bleed

drops of blood

seeping from my soul

forming a puddle

it's strange I'm comforted

by the warmth as I lay here

With the neurotic thought

that I finally know my soul

Crying out with each life

breath seeking an escape

Longing to fly weightless

to secure distinctness

to achieve my eternity

or could this in fact be reality

feeding upon fear

and I'm dying here

Beneath the shadows of thy wings

my soul yearns for peace

but alas I'm transparent

you can hold me

to the sunlight

for close examination

Vanquished Heart

I've had enough
It feels as though

I have nothing left
The world is crumbling
Beneath my feet
All around
The crashing tides of time
Echoes my defeat

Misplaced and disgraced
I have withered away
A broken rose
That never grows
In soil of shattered glass
Why this is so
No one knows

The light diminishes to darkness
A bird with a broken wing
I've tried to fly
Countless times
Alone
But I tumble down
To the ground
And cry
And cry
Asking why

I succumb to the pain

That burns
Inside of me
I lie here
Barely breathing
Feeling
My life
Slip away

The beating of
My broken heart
That lies beneath
My shackled feet
The clanking chains
Echoing my defeat

I've suffered soulless seasons
That once were bright
But the light
That once burned inside of me
Has flickered
Faded
And died

I look in the mirror
And see the darkened aura of my soul
An unfamiliar face
That once was mine
Stares back at me
With eyes full of disgrace
I stand in shadows of this sinister place
Betrayed
By demons once thought slain
I have nothing left

Adrift in a sea of nothingness
How can I escape you
When I can't forget you
Or erase you
From my mind

Your selfish and soulless
A waste of time
Then why
Why God why
Am I the one who's sorry

I taste the bitter tenderness
Of our illusory love story
You left me
Drowning
In a sea of sorrow
My heart
My soul
Was yours to borrow
But now
I lie here with slit wrist pain
Bleeding out

Dying for tomorrow
with Slashes of sadness
Crimson mist that
Pours from my wrists

staining white sands

of a once magical place

now laying in a pool of red

I whisper your name

letting you know

I vanquished my heart

here upon the sands

of our special place

that this my dear
is my last love letter to you

Crimson Red Lips

Consumed by thoughts of you; our love was like fire and slowly turned to ice
Reminders of you everywhere , it seems there is no escaping the memories
Imprisoned is my mind, remembering your touch the way your hand felt in mine
Mirrored by your shadow your silhouette follows me at   times mimicking me
Steaming hot coals burn my hand as I reach out to touch you
Overwhelmed, I'm falling deeper into an ocean of disbelief, I'm drowning trying to escape this despair
Never did I think I would lose my sanity when you left me alone in the cold, fear consumes me
Rendering me still, time goes by ever so slow turning my heart to stone more with each passing day
Everyday feels like an eternity... minutes seem like hours and hours like days and days like years
Dreams of you haunt me, you left an imprint on my soul I'm left sleepless... images of you I see
Reaching out for you but all I grasp is air... I awake screaming out imprisoned by your memory
Like a disease coursing through my veins I was poisoned by your love, I die inside a little more each day
Seasons come and seasons go; I remember the last time I kissed you with crimson red lips in the falling snow

Nights of Darkness

Upon silent wings of night I cry

holding my breath as life takes

bits and pieces away from me

tired of the despair that each waking

hour brings so I long to be lost in shadows

my mind is weak, it's you I seek

your name I try to speak but

I'm choked up like strangulation

it's you I reach for in my dark dreams

and my fingers tremble on keys of pain

I die a little more inside each night

as you look away like you never knew me

as night falls a terror washes over me

because when slumber comes I'm afraid

I'm afraid of dreaming

all I hear are my screams

all I see is my heart bleeding

all I feel is my soul dying

and aching memories dance

around me like sinister clouds

in obscure skies taunting my sleep

hysterical whispers call

my name and I realize

It's your voice haunting me

in shadows I see a translucent

figure pointing blame

silent night...lonely night

let me slumber my pain away

my memories like the rose

of my heart has died

and the thorns purge me

from inside as I cling to life

seeing through shattered eyes

my body washed upon

tattered shores as I realize

This is my beautiful tragedy

I'm left alone to decay

in a cove of loneliness

feeling the layers of pain

being ripped from my skin

so upon silent wings of night

I cry tears of red rain...holding

my breath in sweet surrender

this life of torment has taken its toll

as I long to be lost in shadows

to be dead to the world

rather than be conscious dreading nightfall

my heart breaks in the ocean of my dreams

as I watch my lifeless body

fade out with the night tide

with eyes wide shut and arms out stretched

I can finally accept my fate

Reality of Mental Illness

Alone I sit, a table for one all alone
feeling like all eyes are focused on me
pointing fingers and ridiculing the peculiar looking girl
I was convinced they were all chanting no salvation for the likes of you
So I fixated on the moon as it made its appearance
The only light coming from the moon as it shined down
on this somber mysterious place through an open window
bearing down on my desolate table in the corner
Silently and paranoid, I sat trying to eat my dinner
Yet I did not want any of it
So why did I order it, maybe to satisfy my curiosity
I guess everyone imagines their last meal
nonetheless my mouth did not salivate for it
although I took a bite anyway thinking it would soothe my overwhelmed mind
into thinking this plate of food would be the finest thing I ever ate
So I cut into my steak and put a piece in my mouth
In only seconds I spit it out, not at all what I was expecting
The taste made me sick, smelling and tasting of rancid flesh
staring down at my rice in my mind it resembled maggots
The wine took on the appearance and taste of blood
It seemed like the world was rotting in front of me

I felt as though I could vomit at any minute
So I took my leave to try and rectify the way I felt
Now on to the country cottage by the lake where we used to go on family outings
I had this awful feeling, like my flesh was on fire and melting off of me so
I walked to the grassy banks of the foggy lake the water had an ominous aura
so I leaped into the murky icy water...
WAIT! I yelled out
but my pleas fell on deaf ears, and my body was seized by dead hands of the ones before me
Dragging me down into the profound depths of despair, hearing their screams
mocking me trying to convince me this is the only way out
Maybe I really am insane like the whispers in my mind kept telling me
But never in a million years did I think it would come to this
The last thing I saw were headlights
Just before they turned into the driveway of the cottage
the voice I heard was faint as it called out my name.....too late
This is what goes through the mind on a daily basis of the mentally ill...

Transcendence

Heart as dark as night and cold as stone
forever to dwell alone in the fiery pits of hell
she has gradually lost her grip on reality
alone embracing her dark side
soul dead, her head feels like a bomb about to detonate
not another thought can she bear to think
I was free falling hard without you here
then you came to me out of my dreams my sweet salvation
and saved me, I heard you say in your sultry solemn voice
"I'll be here for you in your time of sorrow
I promise to rescue you from your yesterdays and tomorrows..."
So search your pain look deep within your heart and mind

Always knowing

Always wanting

Always waiting

Brings such pain

Empty lonesome pearl

Spoiled for the wanting

Holding my breath for your careless whispers

Knowing it is time; I don't want to be careful

logical...

boring...

or sane...

No taking it slow and easy

Temporary loss of sanity

Let's let love rescue us

and discover who we are under the darkness of night

with only the light of the silvery

moon to guide our way as we search each others soul

uncovering a love that transcends space and time

Eye Lash Tears

Every rise of the sun, every tic of the clock there is a new memory in my mind to unlock
It feels like I have been frozen in time standing here all these years, when I look at you and in your eyes...
I see my own pain staring back and through mirrored eyes I see the horrible scenes playing out over my life's canvas
I hear these constant words being whispered... but from whom...

I am nobody
who are you?
are you
nobody too?

Constantly you are on my mind, reminders of you everywhere I go
in my head images of you, never did I think I would lose grip on reality

My worst fears arise and take control of my all, consuming my every thought
There is a darkness in me and through my darkness
I search deep within my soul and
I see eyes staring back at me, pain so deep it's hard to swallow, my soul now hallow
I would follow you anywhere to the four corners of the earth and back, if only you had asked

Facing the road ahead I walk a pitch black path
darkness is my salvation
I try to remain strong, but I long for your touch to hear my name fall from your lips
how much more torture can my heart sustain, pain has become my constant companion

I wake nightly tormented by dark dreams it seems they are the only place I feel whole
where you are mine and I am yours, and I can love you freely...

Remembering my dream so vividly and it makes me
wonder were they ever real or just a tortured
fragment of an alluded sick mind
or am I believing in something to real...
as if I were deserving

Fire Embers Burning Slow

I've always kept myself guarded in a glass house

I laugh at the irony of it all now

My battles have always been lost

There's a longing deep within

My flame no longer burns

you made sure to steal it

My arms desolate and cold

My head I carry low to my chest

how else shall I shield it from

this ominous bulls-eye on my chest

I could once more roam the plains

with wounded hands

or just give up and let it go through

realizing there's my heart, a rather pretty

sight, a bright burning soulful expression of love

on fire at the tip of your arrow

just as I knew someday it would

I once told you my love would

always burn for you...well now you have

a trophy of it stuck on your quiver

tell me will you mount it with the rest

or hide it away for your eyes only

as my time comes to its end

I fixated on the smoldering arrow

as I lift my head ever so slightly

from lips dripping blood

I blow you a ring of heart shaped smoke

I at last have satisfaction in knowing

your deed this night will eventually drive you mad

Umbrella Pain

I'll never let you see
the way my broken heart
is hurting me
I have my foolish pride
and know all to well how
to hide away my sorrows
and pain, I do my crying
alone in the rain
sitting under my umbrella
I wish I could give you
my pain for just one fleeting moment
not to hurt you but,
to make you comprehend
how much you hurt me
you promised to catch me
if ever I fell ,alas you did not

the fall shattered my heart

and it lies in pieces beneath

my tree of life and upon

silent wings of night I cry

maybe one day they will

be swept up and put in a jar

and kept on a shelf waiting for repair

but for now leave me alone in my despair

Fade to Black

The darkness fades to light,
as I lay here stranded in a sea of
nothingness
I have no place to go
I have no place to hide
I have no place to rest
And there is not anything in sight...
I am stuck in this...emptiness
Walking around I wonder
when this nothingness will end
no familiarity around me
not a noise nor aroma
Not even one...
there is just me shrouded in blackness
and all I hear is sounds of screaming
my own...hear my torment
sadness fills my soul
feel my turmoil
To much pain remembering
when I used to walk in light
I roam this lonely place and,
this void world has become my home
I stay hidden, waiting...but for what?

Leave Me Alone

Hear what I'm saying, read my lips

Leave me alone in my despair let me drown

to the dark corners of my soul in my own hell I

dwell

It dose not matter what you say or do

Stay away from my sorrow

Stop trying to climb my walls

I don't want anyone around

By chains I am bound and there is simply nothing

you can do

Let my anger and rage have their way as I run

astray

This hell is mine to bare, it's nice that you care

But...there is nothing you can do to make me

smile

not a joke, no words or sentences will help

me from feeling I could not be more lonely

So just stop and hear me

Listen to the pain that courses through every vein within an empty heart, look past eyes that have no soul
My burdens have taken their toll and left me dark, empty and cold as stone

Girl in the Shadows

I'm your shadow

I'm always there

and yet

You never see me

Your eyes are fixed on her

the other one, the better one

With her striking good looks

and her hair of fiery red

she catches your eye

with a mesmerizing stare

and holds it

I stand in the shadow of her

unnoticed

invisible

A shadow within a shadow

Compared to her I'm nothing

Dull

Dreary

Wild black hair

No fiery locks

Dull cloudy eyes

Not emerald green

Why, why would you look at me

When she is there shining

In bright light

A picture perfect silhouette

Entombed Heart

Heart of darkness

soul in seclusion

kindled by your love

amid divulsion

seek refuge inside

one's self

eternal disruption

surrender to me

divine temptation

alone in pain

hear me cry out

through the iron

gates of life

sometimes the strongest

are the ones who

love beyond faults

cry behind closed doors

and fighting battles

nobody knows about

soul entombed nevermore

In Darkness

I await you here in darkness

In sweet abyss

Waiting to control

your every thought

Your every fear it feeds upon

Nothing is what it appears

They say ignorance is bliss

I await you here in darkness

All that you hold dear I clutch

You're sure to miss everything

All your fears it feeds upon

The beast dissolves the bright veneer

A deadly kiss is dealt

Here darkness awaits you

You'll start to disappear and soon

The beast exists you know it

On all fears it feeds upon

No time for tears to be shed

No time to reminisce

Your every fear it feeds upon

Trying to get into your mind

to bind itself to the core

of your inner most fears

If you give in before you know it you'll be gone

without a trace to that dark and dreary place

Where the lonely beast dose dwell "come in " he says in an alluring tone

Be careful don't fall for his tricks or

You will wind up in your own private hell

Eclipse

Sitting here adrift in my own emptiness

gazing about with blistery dead eyes

that once wept tears that stung like

acid rain, into palms of hopelessness

as passers by give looks of disapproval

I can be seen, but feel imperceptible

forced into submission, my spirit broken

my anguished soul descends into the abyss

of hell, the abode of evil entities appear

My body aches , my mind unclear

I try to speak but I make no sound

I'm choked up like strangulation

thick and damp is the air I struggle in

wondering around amongst oddities , remembering

the low down rain clouds, I've snapped, come un-hinged

I'm like a wounded bird with broken wings

I'm caged forced to stay, unwanted and

longing to be emancipated from this

cold to the bone sorrow that binds my soul

to this world keeping my heart in a permanent eclipse

feeling overwhelmed I fight with sweaty hands

to keep a tight grip wrapped around reality

Internal flames burning, smoldering away

returning blood fills a hurt heavy heart

my lungs desperately struggle for oxygen

I'm   exhausted as pain courses through every vein

slow turning seconds tick emotive torture

in conscientious blackness I sit

I'm rooted to this chair

melting into its leather

my brain is aware

that ignorance is bliss

I stare at the glare of false truths

beaming off mirrors of after images

the resonations of your last vibrations

re-play incessantly over and over in my dark dreams

There's nothing to see, nothing to hear

no moonlit nights...

no autumn colored trees...

no singing birds...

no light of day...

unable to hear the rain falling all around me

Entombed evermore

Last Kiss

Her emerald eyes were aglow,

like fire embers dying slow

Head held high she stood tall

with a graceful stance

She moved ever so swiftly mimicking

the dance of a beautiful waltz

Her target she spied,

helpless and serene,

but to her formidable

enemy she remained unseen

she unsheathed her sword

And before he knew it

he was on the ground

in this unfamiliar place

no warning came

not even a sound

A crooked smile

adorned her face

and she gave her

enemy his last embrace

as the face of an angel

gave a bloody eternal kiss

as the blade rings

Her enemies life

had been revoked

after a cold darkness

rests on the forest floor

and with evil stained boots

a once shiny blade

dripping drops of red rain

she remembers her roots

and feels the pain that

a life of an assassin brings.

Cure For a Broken Heart

I've loved you for so long and endured the pain of that lonely love all on my own

Crying tears that left blistered eyes

Why could you not have loved me full-time, perhaps you just could not see

                                                              That maybe I truly belonged

It was not that long ago I rarely said "I Love You" but then I did and also told you

It's been a long time since I've been in love or even thought I could love again

                                                                So
long, in fact

I'm not sure I know what love really is anymore, or if I ever completely knew

I stayed away from love to avoid having to feel anything ever again

                                                                And
keep the hurt at bay

There is a dull ache inside me as I wonder what strange enchantment that has

cast such a cruel spell upon my fate, time it echoes in the wind and mocks me

                                                                You
loiter in my memory

                                                                You
linger in my heart

                                    You
dance in my dreams

I have learned to live with this longing in my heart , I concocted my own remedy

                                    Close
my mind

Breathe

                                    Walk
and Talk

                                    But,
never ever feel...

                              In
essence turn my

emotions off

                                                    and

make my heart of stone

But alas the time has come as I sit here in the dark in the reserve of my alone

feeling like a fool for believing in true happiness I've shut down and take solace in

finding acceptance, more or less that I no longer see you in my dreams

                                                    No more

do I weep for you

                                                    or hear

your voice in my mind

No longer intoxicated with love, just intoxicated to the point of comatose

All the while knowing in the back of my mind it would all become a final fair well

                                                              And
you'd be gone forever

                                                               As
always my love was wrong

                                                               And it
wound up killing me in the

End

Sometimes

Sometimes I turn my back and just walk away

Sometimes I leave home trying to find home another way

Sometimes I fall to the floor regretting things I've said

Sometimes I try and find hope in the things I've read

Sometimes I see your face in someone else's eyes

Sometimes I feel the truth seep through from others lies

Sometimes I doubt my love from things you've said

Sometimes I can't stand the thought of you in my head

Sometimes I want today to be my one last breathe

Sometimes I find a place in my heart where death dose dwell

Sometimes I cure myself with what I should of said

Sometimes I see myself leading the path I should of led

Sometimes I wish I had told you every little thing

Sometimes I try to hold on when I feel I've lost everything

Sometimes I dream of your voice, your whisper on my neck

Sometimes I want to be with you, but think of the past I'd wreck

Sometimes I dream of someone just like you

Sometimes I doubt my reasons why I just can't have you

Sometimes I can see you cry in the wake of my dreams

Sometimes I lie to myself when everything isn't the way it seems

Sometimes I try to help with my selfish acts to succeed

Sometimes I think of the people I'd help if that's the life I'd lead

Sometimes I succeed and give everything away

Sometimes I don't care even if I'd pay

Sometimes I cry for help hoping someone will hear

Sometimes I try to admit it's only death that I fear

Sometimes I end up leaving without saying goodbye

Sometimes I pretend I don't care, but through thoughts I lie

Sometimes I see jealousy in cold remarks I can't reply

Sometimes I see what you've become and it's all a lie

Sometimes I see people with only one thing on their mind

Sometimes I see someone, and loves the only thing they can find

Sometimes I witness love which can't be defined

Sometimes I feel life without you is blind

Sometimes I try to find love in the wrong place

Sometimes I feel love sent though a familiar face

Sometimes I can't find the way to say how I feel about you

Sometimes I see you and know you've missed me too

Beautiful Pain

The heat I feel it rising in me as though I'm on fire and I'm on the inside looking out

I stand in the flames to burn the outside, to stop the burning inside

It's a beautiful kind of pain I'm setting fire to my yesterday to find the light of tomorrow

I'm torn in half in the wake of the burn to make my soul pure to alas be one with myself

For when two souls stand face to face , silently drawing strength and growing stronger

my wings break into fire and I stand in the realm of my true essence

As I am covered in eminent darkness gathered from the infinite depths of pain endured

I let my conscious expand with each life breath and I am infused with a new awareness

and like the eagle, I take flight and soar toward lights of a new horizon and my mind becomes still...clear, and with a new found clarity my vision shines like diminishing storm clouds

and a new is day dawning as I radiate my pain into harmony planting seeds of awareness

to nourish my soul and an inner peace enlightens my thoughts as my crown does shine

finally all is divine and I am once again one with my spirit and I have a heart that can shine

And deep from the center of my being love once lost is now reborn, my heart no longer torn

When Darkness Fell

This is for the one that hurt me, lied to my face

stole my self-respect and made me enraged

there can be no forgiveness for the likes of you, no saving grace

you thought me foolish and blind, but I was ever watchful

but I knew the demons within you and the sins of your heart

you wanted to know my pain and agony, but you could never imagine where it began

I shall show you the hell that await the wicked , the malicious did you think me but a mortal and a mere fool, so much darkness it controls

I am the fallen you chose not to believe in , I lead to either Heaven or Hell , eternally

and my soul is not the understanding of men... as I long for a paradise built out of ashen inferno

The ashes of evil upon the damned ones, I would raise a tower until the fallen have been sated..

my old wounds reopened, my anger yet rages again , ancient wrongs in need of redemption

come dance with me in battle once more, upon scarlet plains

bring your swords and arrows I will show you the path that leads to flames

you have roused my great Dragon to the depths of the underworld my heart is dark and empty because of you and now the sky grows dark and a cold wind blows

as my time approaches , my ties that bind weaken at last...

and though you thought to destroy my beauty, you who do evil, your season will come to pass

my beauty is forever, and in the end you will see, I did not raise the sword first, it was you

when you did not accept me, no compassion shown, I was your victim

but I will not lie down dead, I will stand taller: I will work my spells in shadows,unseen by eyes

calling upon my gods whom you know not exist, high above the clouds gathered in black skies as waters rage on below, in the Abyss, wishing if only I could have been happy and content

a princess in a fairy tale just as you promised saying my being different would not matter

then you turned on me just as I was warned you eventually would, I to naive to believe it's truth

because of your foolish prejudice , Hell must vent... all who hate as you did must lay at my feet

fear the evil my love it's coming, evil begets evil until you are so consumed

Ashen by the fire deprives you of peaceful bliss, I can't weep for those that are self-entombed!

true love will release me from this torment I bear someday but will that love come before the end of time

you never knew my heart's desire nor did you ever care, in turn I never knew you so my heart condemns you to your created prison, the hell you did not believe in or fathom real

your own repentance to reflect in an inferno that has no top or bottom

I did not want to reveal the dark feelings that you imposed on me

but you had to see that it could grow ever stronger when provoked

I had to show you that I was not your equal , no I am superior in every way

do not fear the darkness embrace it my love and be set free

Dream Weaver

I disappear into the blackness from whence I came

I've been living in my own imperfect dream

far beyond a euphoric world, and it's reality

wanting more than anything to wake up

so many times I've tried , but since

you put me in this sleepy trance I just can't

laying here stuck in my own rapture

a permanent stance I am ever so abiding

as my mind you did capture

controlling my every thought

my soul caught and I am trapped

within this world that I have

no authority in, you have a tight

grasp on my days, but you own the nights

Alone in Darkness

Poor lonesome girl with no one beside her

   Dead in my mind and totally blind

   Fear arises and takes control

Alone and cold to the bone

Like ice to her inner core

   Sitting on her throne

   She opened her eyes

As she breathed she could see the frost

   and realized just how empty was her space

   She was alone and prone to nonexistent place

   Utterly sad and crying frozen tears

   her pale expressionless face

   Blood runs from my dark lonely heart

   I've been alone and apart from the world

for so long all she hears is her broken hearted song
Over thinking

  Tired of waiting

  Blood seeps from her eyes

As her imaginary daggers pierce her soul

  Feeling dead inside but,

  Trapped having to show an image of the living

  Falling apart piece by piece

Bit by bit

  She has been used for so long her mind is weary dark and dreary

  Completely imperfect...In a seemingly perfect world

  This loneliness a feeling never to escape

    Cursed to walk this earth alone

Her beloved Prince was taken long ago

Feeling out of place she dose not belong

There is no escape

   Draped in black lace cape

   Crowned with thorns

   Blackened soul

   Destined to dwell in the sewers of hell

   Until her dying day

   Down on bended knee to pray

   that it will be today her end of time is near

Tired cold and utterly alone, so confused

Heart torn in two

Bruised body black and blue

Not recognizing what's true or false anymore

This lonesome and empty feeling

Heavy burdens have taken their toll

she can no longer bear

She just wants it to all go away

No more dose she care

Life or death, no more can she tell

To herself she swore no more pain , she takes the leap

  the time has come to end all

Dark Release

No matter how hard I try to make you remain in the past   and

from my thoughts; you swim through my every vein

Like the pain that bleeds invisibly to my inner core

My heart aches like a slow slaughter

My haunted mind hears your whispers in the dark

You linger in my seeping soul , I swear I'm going stark raving mad

I am caught between hemispheres

I breathe a warm glow of vulnerability

your memory hinders my resistance

I'm in need of redemption from the swirling

temptations in my brain, a release from my dilemma

Pull the dagger from my chest

A minutes rest I'm in dire need of

My sorrow almost pleasure holding me hostage within myself

Is this a test of my will?

In my memory you remain forever

You will always be the desire my body craves

Your love enslaves me and never again shall I be the same

Blackness

Wishes hurt, hellos hurt, everything hurts

Laying on the damp hard ground, tears flowing

I'm broken and lost bound by my pain

I can imagine my spirit leaving my body floating into emptiness

All I feel is cold and darkness my mind wonders with racing thought

Tired of being used as a pawn in the game

I'm alone

I'm unworthy

Why can no one love me

I'm wondering how long this pain I can bare

Descending   into madness within myself

Heart racing in a frenzy and falling apart in bits and pieces

Wishing it would just all end my miserable existence

I can't be rescued I can't be saved there is no hope no future here

I see no light at the end just a dark hole to fall into and be lost forever

Fire and Rage

There's a fire in my mind burning bright, it's flames have reached

the edges of my heart I look down into its eyes, I touch it with burnt

and blistered finger tips...it seeks to mesmerize drawing me in and yes I go willingly

With an infuriating eerie look in my eye let it melt your flesh

hear me as I scream, let the heat embrace your cold and barren heart

until it destroys your bones

Allow my hatred to devour the cruelty that you feed upon

and with a pretty smile on my face flames will rise high

leaving all that you are and all that you see mere ash

Smoke will flow from lips, fire from fingertips

Shades of crimson red with highlighter yellow

will illuminate your many flaws and the scars of your sins

And after the flames of my hatred and rage have consumed you

may it devour my body as well

Free Falling

You make me want to scream until there is silence, darkness I seek

I'm sick of crying I'm tired of trying it's like a horrifying dream

I'm smiling, but inside I'm dying, tears are the words the heart can't speak

My soul hungers for salvation leaving my body weak

To my knees I fall starved for your affection I feel I may parish I want to vanish

I got used to feeling wanted you quenched my thirst by showering me

with your love for awhile it was paradise, then like a thief you stole

that feeling back like it was given to me by accident

Thoughts of you burn my mind like wildfire that no amount of water can extinguish, I once was blind but now I see with eyes wide open

what a liar you really are, alas defeated I surrender unable to fight this losing battle I'm able to rid my mind of you

I've had time to grow and I found my wings and take flight

I vanish out of sight, a life of loneliness my plight I'm free falling with no more self inflicted wounds of pain's strife

Grave Reality

Pieces of light

pierce into my darkness

but shatter upon impact

making my days endless

and my nights silent

no one hears my cries

locked in this metaphorical cage

the darkness consumes

and devours me

tears I shed, blood

from crimson eyes

A soul broken in the

worst of ways

no salvation in sight

my inner light has

faded out of my sight

distance's boundless

wanting to vanish

without a trace

leave this sinister place

that's been drowning me

in nothing but pain

a rage transforming me

I feel it tightening it's

grip on my sanity

a blackness coursing through

my veins, mystifying my mind

slowly driving me insane

my candle is slowly burning out

my hourglass is running out of time

soon I'll be living in the blackness

forever I'll be blind and bound in chains

raging out loud, saturated in bloody rain

the beast will soon break free and

this place I called home will soon be my grave

In my deepness of my dreams it's angles I see

But the reality is I live with demons

Hands of Time

One day you will find a letter

a tattered and crumbled piece

of parchment stained with tears and blood

that have flowed freely from my soul

I have given in, lost all hope

Surrendering to the hands of time

I face a cruel reality and it's hard

to see the face staring back at me

this mirrored image of aging time

youth drained from my flesh

eyes with no soul looking back at me

there is a darkness inside killing me

a slow captivating death

choking my vitality

an all consuming pain to the

bone feeling

Empty is starting to grow

like a withering flower

caught in the shade

All I want is to go away

to a place so far away

somewhere you will

never remember me

and I will not have

to think anymore

about rejection

and the pain of loss

or how it cut

my insides so deeply

Broken Hearted

I once stood in the aura of my love but,
it slowly began to crack and I discovered
you felt it no more and the happiness that
held my smile lost its grip and turned it to a frown
Your words deadly as bullets hit me, and I'm left cold
your footsteps that once eagerly walked to me
are now running fast from me

As you leave...there is nothing worse than the horror felt
than my heart growing colder with each passing day
under dark of night
the wrench of my soul being torn apart, and being reminded
that nothing is forever, not even a love thought unbreakable
the love my life once revolved around... is gone I know
but I am still bound and chained to you by memory
you linger on my lonely mind... and I wish I were the
Tin Man

I weep and fall to my knees for you but yet,
my throat swells up leaving me no air to speak my words
I feel the pain coursing through my every vain
as it all comes back to me, I remember it all
but now it seems to be only an unrealistic dream
my body and my mind feel so tired and used

With all the pain you bestowed upon me I'm
left with questions that have no answers;
why did you wait till I fell in love to leave?
why do I still dream of you?
why does your memory linger?
when will this misery end?

Tell me what wrong I did to make you leave
to make you stop feeling anything for me
or could by some miracle tell me you had a change of heart
and run back into my open arms
are you listening, as I call out your name,
can you hear the beat of my heart
as it grows faint and colder with each passing day

Like a rosebud lying in wait to bloom under dark of night
for the sunlight of a new day dawning...but it does not rise
now you are gone, as if you never existed at all
you left me here to fall apart with a heart shattered
in a million tiny pieces...with unrealistic hope on my mind
but it's the only thing keeping me alive

Sadness is closing in and lies closely by my side
your essence is burned into my soul
and your presence slowly diminishes into cold of night
and I'm left laying alone with bloody hands holding
my heart you ripped from my chest

Her Dismay

Am I dreaming or have I gone insane

lying here on this cold hard ground

bound and chained I'm a slave to your soul

suffering in pain my essence drained

heart torn from my chest

I found a new way to bleed

I can feel you looking directly and

fixedly with a wide-eyed gaze

staring at me as though

you can read my mind

unaware and surrounded

by this all consuming darkness

not meant to see the light of day

from this day forth your prisoner

my days spent in emptiness

my nights spent wondering

and waiting for darkness

to end my dismay

how long will I have

to live in shades of gray

until my existence completely

fades me away to a sea of nothingness

drowning in my despair trying to swim

back to the top, but when I think it

is in my grasp...just a few more feet

a hand greets me to push me

back under my mind in a plunder

once again the devil has his feat

this time I can't beat him

my mind lingers and ponders

did I not used to be happy?

Taken Above

She sits on the

forest floor

to try and find
peace for herself
emptiness abounds

eerie sounds

in moments alone
It's only loneliness felt

She thinks of a love
she can never be his
She wants him beside her
in heavenly bliss

Her eyes saying sorry
she looks at him
He knows her heart

She smiles at him
with a pain

that can never be filled
She feels no more

because there is a hole

where a heart once was
she wants it to end

She thinks he is ok
one day love will find

you anew
He cannot let go
he takes it above

She found him sleeping
He will never wake
Whoever she loves

it seems they are cursed
I'm sorry I made you

my mistake

She takes it above

Dreams of Destruction

I'm afraid of dreaming

all I hear are my screams

all I see is my heart bleeding

all I feel is my soul dying

aching memories dance

around me like dark clouds

in obscure skies taunting my sleep

hysterical whispers calling

my name as I realize

it's your voice that haunts me

in shadows I see a translucent

figure pointing   blame

silent night...let me slumber away

my memories, as the rose of my heart

has died and the thorns purge me

from inside as I cling to life

I see with shattered eyes

my beautiful tragedy

crashing on my tattered shore

leaving me alone to decay

and upon silent wings of night

I cry...
Holding my breath in sweet surrender

this life of torment has taken its toll

and I'm longing to be lost in shadows

my mind grows weak realizing all along

it was you I did seek, your name I try

to speak but it's like hands around

my throat being asphyxiated, it's you I've been

reaching for in my dark dreams

and my fingers tremble on keys of pain

I die a little more each night, as you look

away like you never knew me

and I fade out with the tide

I Told You So

You thought you could repair me a lost dark empty soul

help end my miserable existence

I told you it was useless you insisted on giving it a whirl

And after a few months of giving it a try

You took flight and disappeared far away from me

Just like the one before you

And left me alone to drown in my despair

I wish you would have listened when I insisted and told you

I can't be fixed

I can't be saved

I'm lost tattered and broken my soul lost long ago

Now I sit confined heartbroken once more in a room

of four walls that seem to be closing in on me

To escape I will dream a temporary fix

I take myself to this fantasy land where all is right

and I'm bright and cheery with optimistic views

I wish I could sleep forever

For when I wake it's back to reality

Dark and dreary with no meaning

my heart grows even more weary

The burdens of my mind are more than I can bare I'm weak

Sitting here motionless in my nonexistent space

A blank stare rests upon my face

Memories start to unfold of dreams untold

And takes me back to times of old a place serene and bliss

of countless hours spent daydreaming when I was

happy and carefree

In My Affinity

The room is dark tonight

and I feel trapped

Under sheets of satin and lace

maybe tonight will be

the suffocation of me

once again I cry myself to sleep

and I refuse to relieve the stinging

in my eyes, realizing

I am misunderstand

an unwilling puzzle not wanting

to be put back together

In the realm of my dreams

As I lay here bleeding out among

black storm clouds

I am enveloped by the night

As I free fall into my next breath

there is a deafening silence

the place I plunged in

but oddly in the silence

and the misunderstanding

there is a sweet melody coursing

in my veins, and I never want

it to leave me

no matter how much

life has made me bleed

like ashes under my feet

the remains of nothing...

Slow Burn

It was a slow

and beautiful burn

but the fire

slowly tired out

with nothing

to feed it's

ravenous apatite

and now I rise

like thunder

and break free

of these chains

that bound me

to this despair

And with eyes

wide open I'm

breaking the

window pane

of the past

looking ahead

making choices

which bridge

to cross

and which

to burn

In the fire

of my mind's eye

I seen how

much brighter

life is when...

we focus on

what truly matters...

Listen to your

inner voice

and be brave

enough to follow

your heart

to create your

own magic in life

It is truly ironic

it takes sadness

to appreciate happiness

noise to understand silence

as I sometimes wonder

what is worse

keeping my emotions

locked up

and feeling numb

losing out on

life like love

and happiness

Or to embrace excruciating

pain and along with

every other emotion

that which

makes me smile

and makes your

soul take flight

and feel alive

from every wound

there is a scar

and every scar

has a story to tell

A story that says

I survived pains strife

and through the suffering

and the struggles

I have emerged

with a stronger soul

seared with scars

Holding on to

your anger and rage

is like drinking poison

only expecting

the other person

to die,

But it is I

who am writing

the story of

my life and Captain

of my own ship

and I will no

longer allow

anyone else

to hold the pen

And I have

come to realize

that life always

offers you a

second chance

It's called

TOMORROW....

When I stopped

looming over all

my anger and rage

I was amazed at

how much more life

I have time for

And looking to the

past, I smile

and to myself say

" I never thought

I could do it...

but I did

I overcame all

the people who

tried to bring

me down..."

And from now on

when the wind

blows and whispers

through the trees

and storms

are approaching

while all the other

birds seek shelter

The eagle alone

avoids the storm

by flying above it

So, in the storms

of life My heart

shall soar like

that eagle

and if I still

can't find

my way

all I have

to do

is create one !

Key to a Broken Heart

I have to hand it to you

I got fooled once

memorized all your

hateful words

I should have known

to lay you to waste

but I was desolate

and caved to your lies

so I got fooled twice

and got disgraced by a fool

my selfish pride got the best of me

and wound up on your wild ride

made to feel cheap and unworthy

I'm not claiming innocence

I only have myself to blame

I let you carve my heart from my chest

as we all reap what we sow

I've been down this road

countless times before

this type of hurt my habit

each time hoping for a change

somehow I manage

to put myself back together

I should be happy it all fell apart

I can actually sleep through the night

but what of the lonely nights

when I don't want to sleep

knowing you will consume my dreams

but this time is different, I'm afraid

of the days I don't feel at all

pain courses though my every vain

and it hurts more than it hurts

it burns inside my souls on fire

my mind can no longer walk the wire

I lost my balance lost control and fell

I now dwell alone with a heart that barely beats

standing abandoned on the side lines

watching as life passes me by

I put myself in solitary confinement

behind four walls closing in on me

I've been in isolation so long

can I even remember how to love or

bring myself to trust another

to hold my fragile heart

and put the key in someone's hand.

Lost in You

Somehow I found a way to get lost in you

I thought your tales of love true

little did I know my fall from grace

was so close at hand, I left myself open

for a pain so hurtful, you ripped my beating

heart from my chest holding it in your cold hands

What I saw in you at first light will

forever darken my mind and thoughts

I look in the mirror and see nothing

I feel like replica of my former self

falling to my knees screaming out for you

but it seems they fell upon a self absorbed and uncaring soul

I remember your last glance my way

your eyes were like dark hooks

for the soul, I destroyed myself for

your amusement I fed you my affection

put my trust in you and somehow I let

you define me, burnt bridges for you

but you never seen the anguish

that burned inside of me

I stare out in

the distance and observe

the fires I started

standing here on barren ground

with clenched fists of anger

at the demons I let you

release, you left me here to die

in the middle of nowhere

broken and alone with bowed

head and crushed spirit

reminded of what I really am, nothing

I find myself at a cross roads not knowing

which way to take, unable to remember happy..

Missing

I won't worry sweet one it's a beautiful thing if you could only see

That I will be able to love again one day even though my

heart feels like it's made of ice, shattered in a million pieces

and my soul is broken, my mind is haunted with memories

Maybe with just one sweet kiss you can melt it like fire

and bring me to life, erase the pain I feel inside

I have fallen to the pits of despair my eyes are open but I can't see

trying to remember that in darkness there Is light

Down on my knees crying out, I found a new way to bleed

To my secret door I run to, disappearing forever

I will never go back to the other side, I'm sick of it all

Wishing this was just a cruel dream of mine

and the weight of the world lifted from me

I want to be floating on cloud nine in blue skies

But these imaginary whispers I hear are taking me over

wanting me to lose control, to go missing

Taking over me, I'm going under

Farther away I go my last breath I do breathe

I'm at the end and can never go back

I feel faint, I fade out

I will meet you on the other side

my love...

Did you get what you wanted?

Message in a Bottle

Liquid remedies ease my tormented mind,

it seems constantly I am in a self induced coma

I find salvation in glass bottles, my best friends as of late

They never betrayed me of left me and shield me from the harsh realities of my life

I drown myself   to ease my tormented mind and my sunken soul

To the porcelain God I pray nightly for deliverance from my Evil

Self-induced prayer never tasted so bitter, I hide myself away thinking

Unholy words spoken

still remain

and stain my soul

of pain, I stagger about

I am always running

Left standing alone

in a world so cold

Trying to forget

Sober

Fright Night

H aunted houses

A nd

L unar

L ight

O ld

W icked witches

E vil

E erie

N ight

Fright Night

Tis the night for lunar light

Old haunted houses

And Tricks or treats

A time for kids young and old

to sing and shout

All Hallows Eve

A night that's

sure to bring fright

With black cats that

prance about and

Vampires rising from

their tombs

Witches on magic brooms

that fly the sky

There's ghosts

that loom around

roaming halls

and walking

through walls

going from room to room

Searching for games to play

and watching people

dressed in costumes

and wearing masks

bobbing for apples

and telling spooky tales

All year long we don't dare

to make people stop and stare

But this one night we really

could not care, it's a night

of fun, the only night

it can be done

so paint your face

and get a funny hat

and some of this

and some of that

get a little crazy

just for tonight

It's alright to let magic in

and have some fun

So go ahead and dance all night

Innocence Taken

It's taken most of my life to finally not to judge myself to deal with what happened so many years ago
In my own reasoning you are a twisted abomination who walks this earth, insanity had taken a tight hold of me after your moral indiscretion of taking a young girls innocence and pride and leaving her with feelings of no self no self esteem worth, judgments of myself coming at me like a double edged sword

My moral compass why did I let this happen it was me I blamed.. I have labeled and scrutinized myself through my life's journey of revealing the truth now it's time I write my story down on paper no more to be kept locked in my head ashamed of myself I now know there was nothing I did wrong!

It's what seems a lifetime ago I wish not to keep track of that dark and dreary night from me my body and virtue you took making me feel broken and insecure to this date, I still remember all of my bruises..they still seem fresh vividly intolerable as I revive certain memories.

Black and blue thighs, raw all over, sick to my stomach Left ashamed and alone on that dark lonely country road. For what seems like miles I walked crying in despair a frightened fifteen year old girl what did I do to deserve this is all I could think, how could you violate your own flesh and blood Dear cousin?

When finally home I arrive without notice off to the shower to wash away your stench and the feel of your touch from my body. Not a soul I did tell for fear of being labeled a liar for everyone thought him a hero having been a marine and serving his country if only they knew what a zero you are.

Today I'm lots better, just an unfortunate thing that happened to me. In me used to live a constant battle and now I know I'm not the rape but the journey has taken me through all years. I think myself no longer in pure and a victim, I'm no longer visibly bruised but the black and blues remain in the back of my mind.

And I know I'm a beautiful person when once thought ugly and unworthy of love.. But alas now I love myself again and let others love me. I'm all grown up now and feeling rather content with myself and my new outlook on life has welcomed me with open arms no longer a prisoner of shame..

Ashes of Time

Temperamental tears and devotional swears
Simple minded thoughts that I just didn't care
Justified rights causing disruption in faith
Complication over mindset withdrawing to my fears
Calmed over nerves and a resolution to prayer
I was selfish, screaming to myself that it's just not fair
So with frenzied piercing cries and cold founded tears now wiped away
I'm still left wondering why; so to the heavens I shout in need of a way out
Please Lord I admit that I've lost my way and now I pray
with eyes full of shameful tears I still ask thee why has my love fallen away
Disregard, turning my back to every word you said; I know I made my bed
I just could not find the words to admit the price that you've paid,
is your love lost is this the punishment for my life's crimes being chained to my old ways

Even though I was lost You knew my feigned over life would eventually change
I'm holding on to hope, down on my knees once again
with the sands of time slipping through my hands, hours seem like days
As I scream out to you through clenched fists holding on to the ashes of my time
and on bended knee I plead; help me, I've lost my way, what else can I say
Is all hope lost... did I seal my fate and I realize too late
that my forever love had fallen away
Has your love turned to ash forever lost to me like sands through the hourglass
Then you came to me with hands out stretched... I heard your whisper in the wind
And now with no more doubts or fears I will forever walk with thee

Shadows

Beneath the shadows of thy wings my heart yearns for peace

My shadow looms over me like moonlight across calm waters

My shadow has deserted me and left me empty and hollow

My shadow never gave me warning of it's pending betrayal

it just left me like a cloud of dust on the horizon

My shadow I cry to why now, why desert me now

with each life breath I have sought an escape from you

I long to fly weightless to exist in pure mind

to secure distinctness to achieve my eternity

Is now the time I alas succeed just when I needed

you most, I would have never wished for you to leave

had I known it would hurt this bad

Never did I realize just how much my shadow I did need

Now I am transparent you can hold me to the sunlight

for close examination

My shadow it is hate, it is fear on fear and hate it dose feed

My shadow dose exist because I want it to

I can choose to dispel it or let it keep following me

Ride a Drop of Rain

My heart is heavy, mind in turmoil

I can still feel the last touch of your hand

No one seems to understand

how can I convey everything I feel

wanting to peel all the layers of pain away

The sleepless nights and empty days I'm a mess all alone

I will never be the same your eyes still mirror my soul

No one to talk to since you passed away

the silence is deafening and torment sickens me

The sound of your voice haunts my waking hours

I visit your grave and fall to my knees calling out for you

the night grows cold and memories of you

like rain fall all around me

the cold consumes me as darkness soaks my soul in

I know you are not here but the echo of your essence lingers

and I find solace in knowing you found peace, your saving grace

no longer living in pains strife; that you no longer occupy this dark lonely place

I dwell in my empty space and alas sadness is my shadow

it seems time torments me and my flowing tears taunt me

Spiraling downward descending farther within myself I hide in seclusion

I wish at times I were just dead then I'd be reunited with thee

If only I could go to bed and sleep for an eternity, time a torture for my heart

I'm tired of walking around with a fake smile on my face

I am filled with some happiness knowing our time apart is not forever

Wishing I could grab a drop of rain to ride upon

hoping it would bring me to you..

I AM A POETESS

I am a poetess
nothing more nothing less
and often a quiet mess
The words I write come deep from my heart
secrets I meant to keep
from the world most have no rhyme nor
reason just my random thoughts
So with pen like precious gold in hand to
paper
I can write of it....

The dark moonless night when you left my
side forever
When just yesterday swore you would keep
me warm and safe and never alone
The pain I thought would tear me apart, alone
and deserted
A little easier to bear it makes
I can write of it...
Of days laid day dreaming in one another's
arms
The beautiful times we shared, perfectly
paired were we

Our first kiss, soft warm embrace, in your arms I
found my saving grace, warmth and solace

With a hand so gently placed upon my face
I gaze into your eyes of blue beneath cold of night
Etching face to memory never to be forgotten
Lips meet the taste of sweet love, blissful and serene
Warm breath on skin, eyes closed, I feel as though I've fallen and risen you brought me to new heights, your love delights and enthralls me
I can write of it...
Who knew the next day would feel like hell on earth, I look at myself torn in two
Soul crushed falling to my knees to weep remembering you said my heart you would keep safe
Now I know it was just a heap of lies to get your gain I fell for you game I was your pawn and believed your lame excuses, toyed with like a puppet on a string
Now no one is here to sweep up the pieces of a shattered and tattered heart
as it's turned to stone I'm left alone this pain is my burden to bear all on my own
I can write of it...

For alas I am a poetess...

About The Author

This is the first book of poetry from poet Tammy Harrison, who has been dubbed *The Dark Mistress.*

Her poetry is beautifully deep and hauntingly dark and some have even compared a few of her pieces to Mr. Edgar Allan Poe. Ironically, he has been a major influence since she started writing at the age of 15, winning several competitions in school.

Born in Kansas, she has traveled the whole of the United States as her Father was in the Air Force.

Always with a journal in hand to quote the Author " You never know when an idea will pop in your head so I am always prepared to jot them down..."

           Tammy

Author/Poet Tammy Harrison

www.ingramcontent.com/pod-product-compliance
Lightning Source LLC
Chambersburg PA
CBHW031358040426
42444CB00005B/336